On Fish Stick Money

On Fish Stick Money

Marilyn Whelan

Caviar Living on Fish Stick Money

Library of Congress Control Number: 2015905183

Whelan, Marilyn, Author
Caviar Living on Fish Stick Money
Marilyn Whelan

ISBN: 978-1508958413

BUSINESS & ECONOMICS / Personal Finance / Budgeting

QUANTITY PURCHASES: Schools, companies, professional groups, clubs, and other organizations may qualify for special terms when ordering quantities of this title. For information, email author directly at **moptimist@bellsouth.net.**

This book is printed in the United States of America.

Dedication

Dedicated to my sister,
Diane Friedland.
I can still hear my parents saying,
you have only one sister,
please be close.
Life has taught me
there is no better friend
than a sister,
and there is no better
sister than you.

Introduction

A good friend, upon hearing I was writing a book, asked about my intended audience. I thought about it. I knew my readers could be sitting across from me sharing tea or seated next to me waiting for a flight. Or maybe even a young person about to explore his or her independence. My book would not be the "all-knowing me" dispensing tidbits, but instead the sharing of acquired wisdom.

I believe we mentally write the script of our lives and then proceed to live it. I have always had a bit of a flair for the dramatic. I've always reached out for that special something. I want my life to be exciting and have meaning. I believe it is up to me to make it so.

That does not take a lot of money.

However, it does take imagination, creativity and effort. With practice, it comes easily. First, decide what you want. Then, find a way to make it happen.

When you are about to embark on a journey to a new destination, you don't just get in your car and drive away. You have a road map. The same holds true for the life you design. You create a road map.

I do this with goals. Since childhood, I have written out my goals every year. Then, I revisit them every quarter and review my progress. Having my goals in writing creates accountability. Reviewing them every quarter holds my feet to the fire. I tuck a sheet behind the goal sheet where I list what I have accomplished toward that goal and what I plan to accomplish next.

More people than ever are realizing the value of a balanced, healthy lifestyle. They are recognizing that the awful feeling of being on a perpetual treadmill – the rushed, hectic pace of their lives – is not a normal way to live. They have a choice, and can opt to choose contentment and happiness. They are learning contentment and happiness are not based on accumulating possessions, but in appreciating what they have.

My intent with this book is to share some tips I've developed, and some that others have generously shared, to help you live the good life with less effort and less cash outlay.

I believe in the Law of Attraction. I come from a long line of strong believers on my mother's side. My grandmother's brother, a maverick and family legend, published a book in 1945 titled, "Priceless Personality." In it, he writes, "like attracts like," meaning we attract from life what is deep within our innermost consciousness. To change outer conditions constructively, we must change within. How can we do this? We do this by controlling our thoughts.

By looking at several categories of our lives, we can begin to control our thoughts to focus on the things we want to achieve.

These are the categories I use:
1. Business
2. Community
3. Family
4. Financial
5. Friends
6. Health
7. Household
8. Personal style
9. Personal growth
10. Travel

"Life must be a mixture
of frugality and luxury."
- Marilyn Whelan

The business category focuses on our jobs, paid or unpaid. I am seeing this category in its broadest terms. I am "retired" from the paycheck world, but I see my home and life as a business. I plan with a business plan. I budget as I would with a business.

How successful you are with your business will determine your lifestyle choices. Remember, the key word is "accountability."

First, you must see the big picture. Be organized in every area of your life. Begin with your home. Rid yourself of all clutter. Try to have a place for everything and everything in its place. Taking care of our possessions can be time-consuming. I would rather spend my time doing something more production or fun. At the end of our lives, I don't think our joy will come from how often we dusted or mopped, so consider how much time you want to put into taking care of possessions.

We all make schedules, but be careful you are not just scheduling what you feel you must accomplish in your day. Schedule your life priorities first, before other tasks. Know your goals and life priorities, and make sure you are doing something every day to move yourself along toward what is most important to you. Don't let yourself be so caught up in daily tasks that you lose sight of the big picture.

Take-away tips:

 Treat your home and life as a business, and hold yourself accountable.

 Remember the big picture, and schedule your life priorities before other things.

 Get rid of clutter.

"Go confidently in the direction of your dreams! Live the life you have imagined."
- Henry David Thoreau

"Let us not be satisfied with just giving money. Money is not enough, money can be got, but they need your hearts to love them. So, spread your love everywhere you go."
- Mother Theresa

Community

Our community, in its broadest sense, is our world. We are affected in many ways by what is happening in the world around us.

If you are reading this book, chances are you are lucky enough to be living in a rich, developed country. You have the ability to make many choices.

Our community is our religion, our neighborhood, our schools, our political views. It is all the groups to which we belong. Community is important, because it gives us a sense of togetherness. It offers a framework from which we can learn and grow. Others who share a similar interest can enhance what we can do on our own. We can learn from each other.

Putting our efforts together can help us reach goals we might not reach on our own. A life well-lived includes a commitment to serving others. It is in the realm of community that I develop my volunteer goals. I define and recognize where I want my money and, more importantly, my volunteer time to go.

One of my favorite charities is The Box Project, which matches family sponsors with recipient families. Family sponsors can be families, individuals or groups who want to have a long-term relationship helping and sharing with a recipient family. The sponsors write to their family, get to know the family members, learn from them, mentor them and provide friendship. About once a month, they send boxes of food, clothing, supplies and other material aid to their match family. On average, family sponsors budget about $50 per month for their match family. Some are able to do more; some less.

Perhaps even more important than the goods sponsors send is the mentoring, guidance and friendship sponsor families provide. Sponsors learn as much as they can about their match family, the region, possible services in the area, and other options the recipient family may be able to access. Sponsors encourage and support family members seeking higher education and better jobs, helping the family toward a better level of self-sufficiency.

Sometimes it takes generations for family members to rise out of poverty, and sometimes it won't happen at all, but the role of sponsors is to show that someone in the world cares about the fate of this one family.

Take-away tips:

 Discover a community you can contribute to.

 Make an effort to contribute money or time to something you believe in.

"You don't choose your family.
They are God's gift to you,
as you are to them."
- Desmond Tutu

Family

This category defines your relationships with your significant other, spouse, children, siblings and parents. I plan a "Granny week" every year, when I take some of my grandchildren away on a special vacation without their parents.

I plan and mail surprises to family members who live far away. I plan trips with various family members. I make sure I phone them often. For a year, I watched a sitcom on television because my college-aged granddaughter loved the show and it gave us something to connect about. We had good conversations about the interactions of the characters.

My grandchildren all live far away. Yet we have found a fun way to create a bit of family fun. Every Christmas, I send money in a creative way to the three youngest living in York, PA. One year, each of the three received an ornament made of money. Another year, I carefully cracked and opened walnuts, removed the nut, replaced it with a folded bill and resealed the nut shell. Each one received a bag of nuts and a nutcracker. Of course, not all the nuts held a bill. They had to crack a lot of nuts!

I once unrolled a large roll of toilet tissue, lined it with bills back-to-back, and rerolled and rewrapped the tissue.

Last year, my grandchildren each received a bar of soap with money inside. There were a lot of clean hands that year. Every Christmas day, family and friends call them to see how the money arrived. My oldest grandchild is now in college, and the youngest is thirteen. Four of the grandchildren now are members of a couple. Three are now married. I asked if they thought they were too old now for my unusual money gifts, and they said, "No! Never stop this tradition."

We started a new tradition several years ago. We had a contest among the cousins. I sent each couple a check to cover expenses and told them to see who could come up with the most unusual date.

Couple Number One went on a tour of an old mansion, renewed their marriage vows in the chapel (arranged earlier), had dinner and spent the night out. This grandson is in the military and used his military discounts to stretch his gift.

Couple Number Two went to six locations. They took a large empty picture frame and took photos holding it over the first letter of each establishment. When put side by side, the letters in the photos spelled "Granny."

Couple Number Three ordered a pasta maker attachment for their mixer and made a pasta dinner. They sent photos showing them with strips of pasta almost as tall as they were. They made a great Italian dinner and were proud of the fact they had something to show for their evening. They will remember their grandmother and their fun dinner every time they use their pasta maker.

Couple Number Four learned to drive a dog sled and went on a dog sledding date, followed by hot chocolate.

There were at least fifty judges as everyone near and dear voted. The judges had as much fun as the couples.

The second cousin contest was to see which couple could come up with the most unusual meal. They sent me photos, and let's just say the most unusual meal was definitely unusual. Odd combinations of foods, and food coloring to give the food odd colors, made for a winner.

The last contest was a scavenger hunt in which 100 photos of odd and difficult-to-find items had to be photographed and mailed to me. On the list were things such as a fire truck, a great-great grandmother, a horse and an antique telephone. Everyone had a good time, and that contest provided a first-, second-, third- and fourth-place winner, so every couple got something.

Every family has traditions. Some you bring with you when you make your first home, and some you develop. Traditions provide us with a sense of security and belonging. Your traditions can revolve around meals, holidays or your culture. They could be as simple as a traditional snack or wearing the same color on football nights.

I put small decorations around my home on every holiday. It gives me a festive feeling. I love wearing green on St. Patrick's Day.

Today, many of us have moved away from family, and we have learned to create our families from those we love. We share our good and bad moments with each other. We form bonds as strong as "related" family.

Take-away tips:

 Find fun ways to connect with family members far or near.

 Create your own family traditions.

 Make your own family from those you love.

"Too many people spend money they haven't earned, to buy things they don't want, to impress people they don't like."
- Will Rogers

Financial

I believe each of us should be informed about ways to earn, save, invest, spend and will our resources. Our elders used to say, "Watch your pennies, and the dollars will take care of themselves."

I treat my budget as a business. It is the business of my household. I have learned to stretch every dollar and, in some instances, make every dollar do the work of ten.

As we mature, our lifestyles change and so do our wants and needs. Be careful not to get stuck and make decisions based on what you have always done.

Budgeting

Budgeting does not mean doing without. Think of it as choices. Know the difference between wants and needs. The worst enemy in keeping your spending under control is impulse spending.

I like to keep my budget in Quicken. Quicken has a category called "goals." I first make my budget on paper, then go to Quicken goals and list all my categories. In addition to food, housing, etc., I have both long- and short-term goals. Seeing them in the program is a validation of the goals. I may put only a dollar in some of them at times, and then more when I am more serious about working on that goal.

At the beginning of every month, I enter dollar amounts under the goals. As I dedicate money to particular goals, it no longer shows up as money to spend. When I actually spend toward a goal, I remove that amount from the amount dedicated toward the goal, and "voila" – it is back in my account ledger as an expenditure.

This method is like the old envelope method used by our grandparents, but it's electronic and more difficult to get to the money. Instead of sticking my hand in an envelope to withdraw money, I have to write a check or use my debit card. Using this method, I have a record of my spending. I can easily see where my money has gone.

Saving

One Quicken goal I have is called "overage." At the end of every month, I enter in "overage" the amounts not spent for other goals. At the beginning of the new year, I have a tidy sum in "overage" to spend on something special.

I have another little trick for saving money. When I am spending cash, I use only paper money. If something is $1.01, I hand over two dollars. All change goes into a small money holder, by denomination. When it is full, I roll those coins and place them in a small container. When the container is full, I take it to the bank, deposit the rolls of coins, and enter the amount of that deposit into one of the special goals. You would be surprised how quickly it adds up. It sounds old-fashioned, but it is true that if you watch your pennies, the dollars will add up.

I pay the majority of my bills from the comfort of my home. I have a record I can easily find, and I save on gas, time, stamps and envelopes. I have set up most of my bills on automatic payment schedules.

Credit

Protect your credit rating. It will determine your lifestyle. A good rating will give you lower interest rates and allow you to avail yourself of rare opportunities. When buying a house or automobile, your credit rating will determine the rate of interest you pay. A good rating leaves you with more money in your pocket.

If you are not a traveler, an excellent credit card to use is American Express Blue Cash Everyday which offers 3 percent cash back at supermarkets, 2 percent cash back on gas and department stores, and 1 percent everywhere else you shop. Another good choice is Chase Freedom, which offers a $100 bonus if you spend $500 in three months and 5 percent cash back in rotating categories, such as gas and dining. You have to opt in quarterly, and you have unlimited 1 percent cash back.

Since I travel often, I always choose my credit cards based on airline perks. Using reward points for anything other than airline travel is mostly a waste. My card is paid in full each month. Of course, if you cannot do this, your Number One consideration should be the interest charged. Be alert for airline specials that offer the equivalent of three free trips when you spend a specified amount in a three-month period. If you are close at the end of the three months, but have not yet reached the required amount, you can purchase grocery gift cards to meet the requirement and use them for your food budget.

Mortgages

I am a big believer in owning your own home. When you are a senior and no longer in the work force, it helps to not have a mortgage. Not having a mortgage gives you options It helps to print out an amortization schedule. When you are able to make an extra principle payment, it encourages you to keep going. It becomes a game.

Vehicle Ownership

I have never felt an automobile was a reflection of who I am. I have always viewed a car as strictly transportation. Again, it is matter of choice where you place your priorities. If a new, showy car is what makes you happy and you are making a conscious choice, go for it. Just remember, it is all about choices.

According to the September 2012 issue of Consumer Digest, keeping a car for fifteen years will save you thousands compared with buying a new car every five years. If you drive a car for 200,000 miles and are an average driver, you will have kept the car for fifteen years. This will save you close to $30,000.

Consumer Digest suggests you start with a reliable model, with features that appeal to you and fit your lifestyle. The secret to keeping a car over time is maintenance, maintenance, maintenance. In other words, make sure you take the vehicle in for all the recommended maintenance work.

A site I like to use when I'm preparing to buy is www.TrueCar.com. It offers a free online tool to find a recommended price before speaking with a dealer. You simply enter the make and model, and up pops the average price paid in your area, the factory invoice and the estimated true price. It also will give you the manufac-turer's suggested retail price.

If your car needs repair, call around and comparison shop. Even dealerships within the same area have different prices. Also, www. GasPriceWatch.com can help you find the cheapest gas in your neighborhood.

Passive Income

From the time I was very young, I imagined myself as a landlord. Everyone pays a mort-gage. Either you are paying off a mortgage for yourself or paying off one for your landlord. I have always believed everyone should have some source of passive income. That income might be only interest from money you have in the bank, but passive income is what will make your later years more comfortable.

This where you have to think creatively and imaginatively. Brainstorm, even if with only yourself. Think out loud. I'll give you examples of ways I purchased property, and these were all long before recent housing crises.

A developer of condos went under, and the bank owned the condos. The bank ran a special allowing me to rent for six months and, at the end of the six months, my rent became my down payment. Of course, I had to have the credit rating to qualify.

Another opportunity presented itself when a developer had three liens against him and could not close on a sale. My husband and I made an offer below market value and agreed to bring the unit up to present electrical and plumbing standards if the developer would allow us to rent prior to closing. We knew the developer's liens were small, so we evaluated our risk and concluded the opportunity was worth the risk. We waited four months to close, and when we did all our repairs had been paid for.

Now I am older and have arrived at another stage of life. I no longer want to be a landlord. I am selling my property and am even carrying two of the mortgages. One of my granddaughters, Jenna, is most like me in this aspect. She is in her mid-twenties and already a landlord. She has paid off 75 percent of her property's value.

Take-away tips:

 Know the difference between wants and needs.

 Use "tried and true" methods to put money aside.

 Protect your credit rating.

"I cannot even imagine where I would be today were it not for the handful of friends who have given me a heart full of joy. Let's face it, friends make life a lot more fun."
- Charles R. Swindell

Balance maintaining relationships with old friends and building new friendships. As the song says: new friends are silver; old friends are gold. Seek ways to nourish your friendships. Plan activities, schedule phone calls to those you haven't heard from in a while. Let your friends know how much you appreciate them.

Instead of saying to yourself, "I miss getting together with so-and-so," make a date and put it on the calendar. We have a way of honoring our calendar commitments. Every quarter, I pick a few friends I haven't seen in a while and make arrangements to get together with them.

Everyone loves to give a gift. The right gift, given with thought, makes both the giver and receiver feel good. Plan for spur-of-the-moment gifts, along with those for expected events. You might not know you will need a hostess gift Thursday night, when you are unexpectedly invited to dinner, but you do know when Christmas or a special birthday will arrive.

I always keep a gift drawer. In this drawer are small items I spotted while shopping. They might be on sale or, perhaps, just catch my eye. This drawer is where I go for a spur-of-the-moment gift or maybe to make gift bags for house guests or favors for my card group.

Know how much you want to spend on gift-giving, and make it a part of your budget. It is not fun to welcome January with a struggle to pay off Christmas charges. Plan ahead, and some gifts can be bought or made as the year progresses.

One of my favorite ways to give a gift is to make a themed gift basket. The last one I made was for a friend who had just moved into a new home. She downsized considerably. I made a friendship basket. Each item in the basket had a typed message wrapped with it, which correlated with the item. You can buy shrink wrap at Dollar Tree and give it a finished look.

Another nice, inexpensive gift is something from your kitchen. During the holiday season, everyone loves gifts like plastic spoons dipped in chocolate, wrapped in plastic and tied with a ribbon. Or how about baking mixes in a jar? There are lots of recipes online. Crafts are always fun and, with a bit of thought, show the recipient you really care.

Having fun and doing fun activities should be built into your schedule. That way you make sure having fun is not neglected. I add many fun activities to my calendar. I honor most of them as commitments. Once a week, local newspapers have a section listing local events. Many are free or involve only a small charge. Groupon.com and LivingSocial.com often have coupons for activities at discounted prices. Perhaps some of your friends you have been wanting to see would like to join you.

Offering your services as a volunteer can sometimes get you free admission, so consid er volunteering at a local entertainment venue you enjoy.

Buy movie tickets at up to 40 percent off to sixteen national chains at www.bulktix.com. Many cities have theaters offering second-run movies for a dollar or two. Many national parks are free or offer free days, and you can find them at www.nps.gov. www.couponsforfun. com offers discount coupons to attractions in nineteen states.

The point, again, is to be resourceful. Make memories. Step outside the box.

Take-away tips:

 Make appointments with friends and fun.

 Keep creative gift ideas on your mind
year-round.

 Use online resources to save money.

"What the mind of man can conceive, it can achieve."
- Napoleon Hill

This category involves focusing on diet, fitness and healthy habits. Set goals related to proper nourishment, exercise and mental health. Take baby steps, and work your way up.

At the beginning of the year, determine which physicians and dentists you will be seeing as part of your annual maintenance. When you schedule, space out the visits over different quarters of the year. Put them on your calendar, and keep those doctor and dentist appointments according to your schedule.

If starting a new activity, be careful not to overdo. Start small, and work up. If healthy eating is your goal, perhaps start with selecting one thing to avoid and read all labels to make sure that ingredient is not included. Maybe one meal from scratch a week is a good start for you. Do not set yourself up for failure.

To eat healthier and save money, buy fruits and vegetables that are in season. Find different ways of using them in your diet. There are many recipe sites online. Some of them allow you to enter ingredients you already have on hand to get recipes for creating a meal.

If getting more exercise is your goal, link it to a reward. The reward might be monetary, such as setting aside a small sum to give yourself a special treat. Or you might dock yourself for not meeting goals. You could give a small amount to a charity, writing a check every week if you have not accomplished the goal. Accountability is the key.

Take control of your health, and assume responsibility for healthy living. I use what I call the Earth Gym. The Earth Gym is taking advantage of what is available to you in your everyday life. You might ride a bicycle, or row a boat, or walk for a natural high. Take the stairs instead of the elevator, and park father away from your destination. When going about your daily chores, take a few minutes in the course of your day to do a few yoga exercises or even aerobic ones.

Keep a healthy attitude. There is a mind-body connection. I once visited a Chinese physician in China, and he explained that the major difference between the Western and Eastern philosophies of health care is that the Western world puts out fires when disease is present and the Eastern method concentrates on preventing disease. As in all areas of living, strive toward balance.

There is a time and place for home remedies. Chicken soup is a miracle cure for whatever ails you. All joking aside, you might try a simple remedy first. Hot tea and honey for a cold or sore throat might do the trick. Of course, if you are still suffering, it may be time to see a physician.

Take-away tips:

 When it comes to new physical activities, start conservatively and build up.

 Keep a good maintenance schedule for your body, like you would any other valuable piece of equipment.

 Balance prevention and cure.

"The winners in life treat their body as if it were a magnificent spacecraft that gives them the finest transportation and endurance for their lives."
                                          - Dennis Waitle

"The most substantial
people are the most frugal,
and make the least show,
and live at the least expense."
- Francis Moore

Household

This category is related to maintaining and enhancing your surroundings. It is here that I have goals such as eliminating clutter, cooking two days a month to fill my freezer, and making my home a relaxing and inviting retreat.

Eliminate Clutter

Living with simplicity is a lifestyle I am trying hard to embrace. Too much of our time is consumed with activities related to being a caregiver or custodian of our THINGS. Clearing out your collection of things is defining. It frees up time that can be spent in better ways.

Feng shui principles teach us to clear our path. This applies to your home as well. Taking care of your things is time- and energy-consuming. Our time and energy are limited. Think of them as resources helping you live the life you desire. How much of your day are you willing to give to maintaining possessions?

I am not advocating you live the lifestyle of a monk, just that you live in a state of awareness. Choose what you need to make you feel complete.

I've had the opportunity several times to live with limited things. My husband and I used to travel the country in a travel trailer. We roamed Europe renting small apartments for short periods.

Simplify

Simple living does not mean moving to a cabin in the woods, living off the grid, or forgoing plumbing and electricity. It means making conscious choices. It means knowing the difference between a want and a need. One can live simply in the lap of luxury. You can have anything you want; you just cannot have it all.

You have to make conscious decisions to work toward those things you value.

Learn to think in terms of labor hours. When shopping for a dress, for example, break down the number of hours you must work to buy that dress. Do this for every larger purchase.

Ask yourself if you are willing to trade 10 hours of labor for the dress, and if you would willingly do so, buy it. Ask yourself if that big house or car is worth the hours you put into that job. Or has it taken away your freedom? Does it tie you to a job you do not really like?

How many of us have knick-knacks around that we really do not want or even like, but a favorite niece or nephew, an elderly aunt, a friend or a neighbor gave them to us, and we do not want to hurt their feelings?

Look around your kitchen. Most of us see gadgets that do a very specialized task. I try to buy something that will do the work of several of those gadgets. I used to buy canned air to clean my computer keyboard until someone suggested a turkey baster. It does the job quite well.

I love the European style of sleeping on only a bottom sheet and using a duvet. I change the bottom sheet weekly, but flip over the duvet. That is laundered every other week.

To live simply, you must be organized. Having traveled extensively in a small travel trailer, I've learned that everything has its place and when I use something I have to return it to that place.

Towels, for instance, can be folded in and rolled for storage. Select one or two colors, and weed out the odd towels that used to match something, but no longer do. Donate them to a pet shelter.

Sheets can be folded and placed in one of their matching pillow cases. In your closet, you'll be able to spot the set you want and grab the entire set. There will be no looking for the pillowcases or matching sheet.

Decorating

I love holidays and special events. It gives me chances to add a little sparkle to my home. I once made a white tablecloth with pieces of Velcro distributed at different levels around the sides of the tablecloth. I then made sets of felt-based decorations to fit holidays or a birthday. When the occasion arrived, I simply applied the appropriate set of decorations.

I keep a box of decorations for each holiday, purchased, of course, at the end of that holiday in previous years. I don't overdo, but showcase favorites to brighten the mood.

If you are seeking a starting point in your journey to the life you want to live, start with ridding yourself of clutter. Clutter in your mind, your home or your work environment will drag you down. And I mean down in deep doo-doo.

By the time most of us have dealt with daily clutter, our initial energy is gone. Instead of working toward our goals, we are wasting our precious time and energy dealing with the clutter of life.

Try hard not to be the one who has to have the latest and newest "whatever" that Madison Avenue is promoting. Great savings come to he who waits.

Meal Planning

Bread is the staff of life. Some of us are satisfied with whatever our hand reaches on the bread shelf at the supermarket, while some examine labels for nutritional value or simply price tags. My style is once-a-week grocery shopping.

When the newspaper ads come out on Wednesdays, I see first what the loss leaders are. These are the items the store advertises to draw you into the store. Many of those items are buy-one-get one. From the ads, I make a tentative list and add those items I need to replace or need for a specific recipe. I do use coupons, but clip them only as needed.

There are many websites today that match coupons with the specials at your favorite grocery or drug store. It is like having someone do the work for you.

I shop at only one store. I pick the one I believe will give me the best value. I do not plan my meals until I have shopped. I plan my meals around my purchases.

If I had to pick only one tip for controlling the food budget, I would pick a freezer. Yes, I live in a condo, but I have the smallest possible freezer in my guest room covered with a nice cloth and several decorative items on top. If this sounds like a lot of work, remember that I work from my kitchen fridge and use the freezer only for longer-term storage.

My favorite item in the kitchen is my large crock pot. With crock pot cooking, meat is always tender and flavors always well-blended. My secret for easy, creative living is this: When I cook, I try to make enough for several meals. It is not much more work to peel a few more potatoes or chop a few more vegetables. I then divide the dish into portions and freeze the additional meals.

When I know I will be away all day and coming home tired, I just go to my freezer in the morning and pull out my dinner. While I'm away, it thaws. Cooking in this style lends to trying more creative and new recipes. You see something on sale, look in your cookbooks or online, and find a recipe you'd like to try.

Setting your table in a festive manner can create an ambiance guests remember. Dollar Stores offer fun items for this purpose.

Take-away tips:

 De-clutter.

 Figure out the labor hours required to buy and maintain possessions.

 Plan ahead.

"The home should be the treasure chest of living."

\- Le Corbusier

"Fashion is about dressing according to what is fashionable. Style is more about being yourself."
- Oscar de la Renta

Personal Style

This category is about developing your own personal style and enhancing your self-image.

Clothing

Your clothes should reflect your lifestyle. Clothes are to you what a frame is to a picture. People make judgments about others in fewer than thirty seconds. You may read this and chuckle, and say to yourself, "So what?" But we do, in subtle ways, sometimes need the approval of others.

Life is much easier if people react to us as we would like them to. Regardless of whether we are facing our child's teacher, interviewing for a job, renting an apartment, or just spending a day browsing thrift stores, life is easier if we portray ourselves in a certain way.

Take a look at your closet as you think of where your time is spent in a typical week. Think of it in percentage terms. If 70 percent of your time is spent working in a business atmosphere, 20 percent at play, 5 percent partying and 5 percent in a religious setting, let your wardrobe reflect that. Your closet then would be 80 percent business suits or office attire; 20 percent jeans, shorts and casual wear; and a few dresses and gowns tucked in the back for formal occasions.

Think of who you really are. What image do you want to portray? Identify your type. If there were no obstacles in your way, would you like to portray yourself as elegant, trendy, hippie, classical, outdoorsy, a fashion plate, feminine or a mixture of theses? Once your picture is clearly defined, work toward refining that image. Make it fit your lifestyle.

If you know your style is classic elegance, pass up the lace-and-ruffles blouse offered at 90 percent off. Maybe it is cute, and a great buy, but if it is not your style, it will hang in the back of your closet. One of my granddaughters once told me I like gypsy frou-frou. I agree. I do like gypsy frou-frou. I just have to make that style work for me.

Once you have identified your style, you can adapt that style to look elegant, outdoorsy or casual, as the occasion demands. You can dress up or dress down your own unique style. With adaptation, your style will always reflect you.

Think in terms of three when putting together outfits. You might color coordinate two of them or portray a style, but it is the third piece that pulls it together. The third piece – the final touch – adds flair. It might be a flower, a piece of jewelry, a scarf or a jacket, but it will be the finishing touch.

If you splurge, splurge on a basic element of your wardrobe that will not go out of style. Make it something you can live with for a long time – something that can be used in a variety of ways, such as a jacket.

Know the colors that flatter you. Turquoise and coral were bridesmaids' colors for many years, because they are the only two colors that look good on everyone. I suggest you pick three colors as your wardrobe staples. Mine are black, white and red. When you buy something new, make sure it goes with at least two of your three colors. This works well when you have to pack for a trip as well.

Most of us have wonderful garments in our closet that have been hanging there for some time, many with the tags still on them. Maybe we never found the right blouse or skirt to match, or maybe we were waiting to lose weight. Or perhaps the right occasion never arose.

Be a bit crafty to augment your wardrobe. A walk through one of the major craft stores will give you lots of ideas. Painted flowers on a sweater or blouse can lift the ordinary to the extraordinary. Buttons can be art. Simple embroidery can give an item an expensive look.

Be relentless in organizing and cleaning out your closet. Hang your clothes according to type and color. There are many do-it-yourself closet organizing tools. Create the system that works for you. Your unloved, disastrous choice could be a favorite for someone else. Get rid of it! If later you find you have a use for something you got rid of, chalk it up to having an organized closet and move on.

I attended my first clothing exchange party this year, and I can see why this concept has become so popular. A service sorority sponsored the event, and about twenty-five people attended. For the sorority, this has become an annual event.

The hostess had three very large clothing racks marked, "small," "medium" and "large." She had a hat rack for purses, a table for shoes, and a velvet backdrop for jewelry. One of the members asked each of us who attended how many items we brought, and we were given that number of tickets.

All items had to be in good shape; many still had tags. We were given a few minutes to browse and then invited into the den to visit and enjoy refreshments while our hostess called numbers from tickets in a basket. She called only three at a time. Those of us with the matching tickets were told to "go shopping."

Each ticket allowed us to select one item.

It was such fun, and afterward we were all allowed to browse and select anything else we wanted. All leftovers were then given to a shelter for abused women.

Cosmetics

Women spend millions of dollars a year on cosmetics. Are they getting their money's worth? We are bombarded by advertisements and commercials from the beauty industry. Companies walk a fine line: Their claims need to be suggestive enough to ensnare consumers, but not so explicit they get nabbed by regulators. Their seductive words help you see mental images of the artful change that will take place when you use these products.

Is there a difference between day creams, night creams and moisturizing agents? Is it worth it to pay more for a very expensive brand versus a drug store brand? How about various creams for different ages? Is there a difference?

There is little scientific evidence for many of the claims made. Generically speaking, lubricants help smooth dry skin that is rough and flaky, giving it a silkier feel. All creams are an "emulsion" of a water base and an oil base with an "emulsifier agent" to bind the two so they will not separate.

The basic difference between a cream and a lotion is the percentage of various oils and water base used. Since much of the benefit is emotional, the container is crucial for that luxurious feeling. Almost all the expensive cosmetic lines have inexpensive lines; the difference when a product comes off the assembly line is the container. Treat yourself to a nice crystal or china container, and use it to hold the product you like. It will spruce up your dressing table and bring a smile to your face.

Two of the most effective things you can do for your skin are to stay out of the sun as much as possible and wear sunscreen. Drinking plenty of water also helps keep your skin looking healthy.

Take-away tips:

 Know your style, and be creative about adapting it to various settings.

"Life isn't about finding yourself; it's about creating yourself."
- George Bernard Shaw

Personal Growth

This category is about renewing yourself. This is where you can add new dimensions and diversity to your lifestyle. It is about developing goals to enhance your creative and intellectual abilities.

Learning

Reading "books for dummies" is a good way to start learning about something new. Or find someone with the know-how, and offer to trade one of your skills or services for lessons. Ask if you can observe an expert as he or she works.

To expand your knowledge, join a special

interest club. Most welcome beginners. The world is your oyster. Open it up!

When you live a creative life, you are always learning. And your learning can be through both formal and informal channels. You can sign up for a class with other students or self-direct your own exploration.

You can find thousands of free classes with Open Education Consortium www.oeconsortium.org. Also, the Massachusetts Institute of Technology (MIT) available now .offers more than 1,800 courses, which you can see at ocw.mit.edu.

The British Broadcasting Corporation (BBC) has tutorials about French, Spanish and Mandarin at www.bbc.co.uk/schools/primarylanguages. [

Www.coursera.com offers hundreds of on-line classes from many top universities and organizations. All these avenues offer you a path toward your own personal growth. Learning activities will keep you sharp and could help your career. You will be energized being around other lifelong learners. Stretch yourself. Grow.

Hobbies

Hobbies enrich your life. They can be practical activities such as cooking, sewing or building. You can experience the joy of creating something from scratch, and you will own something like no other in the world.

A hobby can involve learning a new skill, language or technology. It could lead to a better job or help you develop a side job. Jigsaw and other types of puzzles or Sudoku can keep your brain active.

Working on a hobby can be a form of relaxation. It can even be a form of meditation, in which you lose yourself in what you're doing. Your hobby could lead to new friendships as you seek out others who share your interests. A hobby can go a long way in keeping you healthy.

I have used Groupon.com and LivingSocial. com to explore various interests. Right now, I have my eye on a four-week class in wearable art. Pinterest.com also can provide ideas to expand on, or introduce you to, new concepts.

Reading is one of my all-time favorite hobbies. I almost always have a book with me, either on my iPad or in print. If I had nothing else to read, I would read labels on medicine bottles.

My favorite book site is www.paperback-swap.com. There you can order printed books you can exchange through a point system. If your desired book is not available there yet, you can enter it on a wish list and be notified when a member has posted it. There is a helpful page that tells you how much postage is required and even prints it out for a small fee.

Www.jungle-search.com/uskindle.php helps you search through more than 3,000 e-books. It is free to download the Kindle app for your computer, and many sites offer free e-books, such as www.hundredzeros.com. Ereader News Today will send many choices each day of which a number will be free.

Www.free-eBooks.net offers no-cost books from new and independent writers. Barnes & Noble offers more than 2 million digital titles for sale at www.bn.com.

Technology

Sometimes I think I am having a love affair with my computer. It has opened so many doors for me. I love email, because it keeps me in touch with friends and family. I have joined so many interest-related newsletters. They teach me new things or reinforce my chosen lifestyle. When my computer has to be repaired and is out of commission for a few days, I am lost.

I like Facebook because it allows me to keep in touch with so many friends and family. I like seeing the photos and reading the doings. It is a way of keeping in touch. Please, however, do not put intensely personal things on Facebook. They have a way of coming back to haunt you.

Donna Tapeline, the electronics guru from Shop Smart Consumer Reports, says you do not need to spend a lot of money keeping your computer safe from viruses. She says free security software provides plenty of protection for most of us, and there are several free options available. She recommends Avira Antiviral Personal at www.avira.com/free.

Spirituality

To be spiritual is not necessarily to be religious in the traditional sense. You can be spiritual through your religion or through a personal transformation. For me, it is a feeling of "walking with God," a feeling of oneness with the world. It is like being high on life. It is a feeling of being connected with your surroundings and feeling that connection with all those sharing your world. When in that zone, you strive to be your best self.

"If we did the things we are capable of, we would astound ourselves."
- Thomas Edison

Take-away tips:

 Always continue learning.

 Take care of your spirit.

"Be not afraid of growing
slowly—be afraid of
only standing still."
- Chinese Proverb

"The world is a book,
and those who do not travel
read only a page."
- Saint Augustine

Travel

Travel is and always will be my passion. My vacations are planned around volunteering, family, adventure, learning and fun. As long as I can be warm, I am willing to go anywhere at any time. I have had the good luck to experience many different types of getaways.

Volunteer Travel

Because my husband was retired military, this allowed us to travel on military cargo planes. We often would sign up for five destinations and take the first one offered. Our main objective was to cross the ocean. We traveled often to Spain, Italy, Germany and England and branched out from there.

We served a tour of duty in the United States Peace Corps. We served in the Philippines, and I still keep up with good friends we made there. Many people do not realize Peace Corps volunteers are drawn mostly from two groups: people fresh out of college and retirees.

There are many wonderful opportunities for volunteer-oriented vacations. Perhaps you'd like to try an archeological dig, or pulling weeds on a mountain trail, or counting turtles on a distant island.

One of my favorite adventures was a month I spent volunteering for the National Park Service at Andersonville, GA. Andersonville was the site of the largest prisoner of war camp in the South for Union soldiers during the Civil War. It is now a national park that includes a museum devoted to POWs from all of America's wars. I was a greeter in the museum, helping visitors look up their ancestors, and I sometimes helped in the gift shop. My two days off per week were spent touring the area. While I was there, I stayed in a small cottage in the cemetery. I was the only one on the grounds at night. It gave me lots of time to reflect, and I took several projects with me to work on. There was no television reception in the area, nor did I have Internet access.

My second-favorite volunteer location was with Pueblo Ingles. This is a for-profit agency that helps Spanish executives perfect their English. For the Spaniards, it is a very expensive program paid for by their employers. The program does not accept participants who speak only Spanish, because the goal is for them to totally immerse themselves in English. Once you are accepted into the program as a volunteer, you work with program personnel to select a date. If you're coming with friends, they work with you to offer a week to your party as a group.

We paid only for airfare. We were met in Madrid the evening before departure for the resort and taken to a banquet and flamenco show with our fellow Anglos. Anglos come from all English-speaking countries, such as the U.S., England, Ireland, Wales and South Africa.

The next day we were taken by bus about 2 1/2 hours from Madrid into the mountains near the Portugal border. The resort was beautiful. Each of us was assigned with a Spaniard to a casita with a bedroom and bath for the Spaniard upstairs and a bedroom and bath downstairs for the volunteer. We shared a small living room and kitchen area. A chef prepared three meals a day, with wine accompanying lunch and dinner. It truly was an unforgettable week for a lifetime of memories. You can learn about this program at www.diverbo.com/en/jobs.

Vacations are for fun, excitement and trying something new. Consider participating on a cattle drive. Dryhead Ranch in Montana is a working cattle and guest ranch. One of the most popular activities there is driving the cattle 50 miles on Bad Pass Trail. This is a three-hour drive that gives you to chance to get acquainted with the beautiful Montana country. For more information, go to www.dryheadranch.com.

Packing

Getting a trip off to a great start can be as simple as packing correctly. A list is essential.

It helps to have a master list to start from. On this list are the items you are most likely to need wherever you go, such as an alarm clock, camera, cell phone charger, medication, small flashlight or night light. Give thought to what your days and nights will entail. Think of the things that will bring you comfort and ease.

When planning clothes, select only three colors that will go with each other. Make sure you have both solid and patterned bottoms and tops. Choose items that go with more than one other item. My rule is that each top must go with three things. Roll your clothes. They will take less room and are less likely to wrinkle.

Consider the mood of the vacation when you pack. Will it be an exciting adventure, casual down time, family event? Choose your clothes accordingly. Have a plan. Your trip plan doesn't have to be written in stone; it can be changed along the way. But have a plan for the things you think you want to do or see. That said, be open to changes in the plan. Be flexible.

Souvenirs

When shopping for souvenirs, consider adding a special piece to your wardrobe or buy something for your home you can incorporate into your decorating scheme. Make it authentic – something a craftsman made or a work of art. Let it remind you of the wonderful trip you took. You want to look at it for years and smile. I often carry my purchases on the plane with me. I feel like I can replace my clothes if lost, but not my special remembrances.

Travel Deals

Vacations do not have to be costly. Thanks to technology, you have more tools than ever to nab the best price for a great getaway. These tips will help you save time and money, both when searching for deals and while you're actually traveling:

- When purchasing airfare, try to be flexible about your travel days for a lower fare.
- Consider buying early. If you must travel during peak travel times, such as when school is out or over Christmas or Easter

vacation, buy as early as possible. Airline ticket prices typically go up in the
last two weeks before flying.

- Consider buying late. This is major risk,
but sometimes airlines have open seats
at the last minute and offer them in
newsletters to their loyal flyers. A simple
online search will help you find the
cheapest days to fly.

- Shop around. Always, always check
as many prices as time permits. Never
book the first price you see. A small
sampling of sites to check includes
www.priceline.com, www.orbitz.com,
www.travelzoo.com, www.kayak.com/
flights, www.expedia.com, and www.
farecompare.com. These sites will help
you figure out which airlines fly to your
destination. Next, you can go to the
website of the airline with the lowest
fare and check it directly. Maybe that
airline will offer a special sale or pro-
motion, or maybe you can just hit the
site at the right time.

- Be flexible. If you live near more than

one airport, check out fares from all the airports near you. Many online fare-searching engines will ask you if you are willing to depart from or arrive in alternative cities.

- You'll usually find the lowest fares for travel if you look on Tuesdays, Wednesdays and Saturdays. Also try to fly mid-week, which is less costly. Prices on the Internet are lower for car rentals, hotels and flights. You can compare prices among Travelocity, Expedia and Orbitz.

- Peak seasons are tricky. Often flying the week before or the week after a peak season can make a huge difference. I remember once taking a cruise to Alaska the last week of the peak season. It turned out to be the warmest week of that season.

- When renting a car, www.AutoSlash. com can tell you when a good deal comes along. Check for coupons and specials. This site will track your reservation and alert you when a special deal is offered.

- When buying travel insurance, try a multi-insurance site such as www. insuremytrip.com. Don't buy insurance from a tour operator, travel agency or cruise line. They work with only one agency and may use the one that offers them the highest commission rather than the one that best meets your needs.
- For booking a hotel room last-minute, download an app called Hotel Tonight. It not only gives you up to 70 percent off, but you can check availability a week in advance.
- Have an RV? For a $35 annual fee, you can park free overnight at one of 351 farms or wineries. Find out more at www.harvesthosts.com. For free or nearly free RV campgrounds, try www. freecampgrounds.com.
- Satisfied with only a place to lay your head? Consider a Pod Hotel. Arabella Bowen, executive director for Fodor's travel likens the pods to cruise cabins. After all, most travelers do not spend a lot of time in their rooms, but consider

the hotel a place to be comfortable at night. Pod Hotels can be found in many foreign countries and also airports such as Atlanta and Heathrow. One example is Tubo Hotel in Tepoztlan, Mexico, where you sleep in a recycled drainage pipe. All rooms have a queen-size bed, light, fan and Wi-Fi. There is a swimming pool on the grounds. A package plan is offered for cooking lessons with fabulous celebrity chef, Ana Garcia, the Mexican Rachel Ray. Check it out at www.Tubohotel.com.

- Italy's newest high-speed trains, Italo, advertise larger windows, wider seats, more elbow room, smoke-free and air conditioned cars, and Wi-Fi. Find out more at www.raileurope.com.
- When planning a trip, check online for free activities. Many regions and cities offer free concerts in the park, lectures in the library and ranger-led walks, just to name a few. While online, check for discounted tickets and special deals. Look on www.restaurant.com for dis-

counts on meals.

- Military families, both active duty and retired, can fly "space available" to foreign countries. They can stay on bases in short-term housing in the U.S. and abroad. Most bases have a ticket and tour office where discounted tickets are available. I recently went with several friends to the Naval Base in Key West where we had a reservation for a three-bedroom house for four days. It was wonderful, complete with a fully equipped kitchen and all linens.

Tax Advantages

While my goal is not to give tax advice, you can often take advantage of having Uncle Sam pay for part of your trip. Suppose you want to buy a boat and "sail the ocean blue." In addition to your home mortgage taxes and interest, you may be able to deduct a second home mortgage taxes and interest. If the boat of your dreams has sleeping and cooking quarters and a bathroom, it could qualify as a second home. This also holds true for a travel trailer or motor home.

If you are traveling to an exotic location for a volunteer experience with an accredited organization, you may be able to deduct the cost of your travel expenses, as long as the volunteer work is the primary reason for your expense.

One such trip I found recently is offered by the Unitarian Universalist Service Committee. It could be considered both a service and a learning vacation. The committee is partnering with BorderLinks. BorderLinks is a binational, nonprofit educational organization at the U.S.-Mexico border. The organization focuses on cross-border relationship-building opportunities, immigration issues, community formation and development, and social justice in the borderlands between Mexico, the United States, and beyond.

BorderLinks has extensive experience designing programs, and nearly 1,000 individuals participate annually in BorderLinks learning opportunities. Volunteers have the opportunity to meet with Immigration and Customs Enforcement, go on a desert walk, and participate in a discussion with a public defender.

Other ideas are provided below. Many of

these organizations charge a fee, but others are free:

- Want to learn to speak a foreign language? Your course may be offset by the lifetime learning tax credit worth up to $2,000.
- One-day cooking classes in Europe can be found at www.theinternationalkitchen.com.
- Many foreign countries have English-speaking volunteer greeters who belong to the Global Greeter Network. Find it at www.globalgreeternetwork.com. The greeters are not trained guides, but will spend a few hours with you introducing you to native haunts.
- Dublin is known as the City of a Thousand Welcomes. It matches first-time visitors with volunteers for a cup of tea or a pint. Find information at www.cityofathousandwelcomes.com.
- The folks at www.meetingthefrench.com organize dinners in private homes in Paris.
- Find Couchserfing.com which takes you to a facebook application whereby you

can join and stay with locals instead of at hotels.

Flexibility and Resourcefulness

You don't always get everything you desire in accommodations. When I scheduled three weeks in the Berkshires with a friend, we had a great timeshare with two bedrooms and two baths. The operators obviously did not want visitors to do a lot of cooking, because the kitchen had only a small refrigerator, a very small microwave and a sink. It was a bit of a shock, since we had not counted on eating three meals a day in restaurants for three weeks. We went to a local Kmart and purchased an electric hot plate and a set of three pans. We shopped local farmers' markets for produce. By being flexible and resourceful, we ended up preparing meals that were gourmet quality.

"Travel is fatal to prejudice, bigotry, and narrow mindedness, and many of our people need it sorely on these accounts. Broad, wholesome, charitable views of men and things cannot be acquired by vegetating in one littlecorner of the earth all one's lifetime."
- Mark Twain

Conclusion

Balance is critical in life and will do more for creating "wealth" than anything else. I have found family, friends and travel to be more valuable than anything else. Savings and good money management allow me to spend more time with family and friends. Creative vacationing has allowed me to travel to new places and learn new things, as well as build a wealth of relationships along the way. I truly live a "caviar" life. I hope you will take advantage of these tips and be empowered to do the same.

Resources

Community Service
The Box Project
www.boxproject.org
800-268-9928
315 Losher Street, Suite 100
Hernando, MS 38632

Computer Security
- Avira.com/free: Free personal Antivirus software

Entertainment

- Bulktix.com: Movie tickets for up to 40 percent off
- Nps.gov: National Park free days
- Couponsforfun.com: Coupons for local attractions
- Kidsbowlfree.com: Bowling deals for kids
- Groupon.com: Coupons for all kinds of activities
- LivingSocial.com: Coupons to explore an interest
- Restaurant.com: discounts on meals

General

- Pinterest.com: Ideas for fashion, beauty, home décor and more
- Meetup.com: A ton of special interest groups

Learning

- Oeconsortium.org: Open Education Consortium offers online classes from around the world
- Ocw.mit.edu/index.htm: offers more than 1,800 courses at MIT

Reading

- Paperbackswap.com: Order books with a point system exchange.
- Jungle-search.com/uskindle.php: Helps you search for Kindle books.
- Bn.com: More than 2 million digital titles
- Hundredzeros.com: Zero dollar books
- EReader News Today offers a list that is e mailed every evening with about 20n free choices.
- Free-eBooks.net: Offers no-cost books from new and independent writers.

Travel

Flights:
- Priceline.com
- Orbitz.com
- Travelzoo.com
- Kayak.com/flights
- Expedia.com
- Farecompare.com

Car rental:
- AutoSlash.com

Trip insurance:

- Insuremytrip.com

Travel Opportunities:

- Globalgreeternetwork.com: Worldwide greeting program
- Cityofathousandwelcomes.com: Dublin guides
- CosyFinland.com: Learn about Finland from Finnish people
- MeetingtheFrench.com: Many local
- offerings in Paris
- Harvesthosts.com: Free camping sites for RVs
- FreeCampgrounds.com: Free camping
- sites for RVs
- Dryheadranch.com: Dude ranch
- experience
- TheInternationalKitchen.com: Cooking
- vacations and one-day courses
- Servas.org: international network of hosts and travelers

Vehicles

- TrueCar.com: Find out what your car is worth.
- GasPriceWatch.com: Find the cheapest gas price.